This
DRAWN
& QUARTERED
MOON

{POEMS}
klipschutz

anviL
PRESS

LIBRARY AND ARCHIVES CANADA CATALOGUING IN PUBLICATION

klipschutz
    This drawn & quartered moon / klipschutz.

Poems.
ISBN: 978-1-927380-45-1
    I. Title.

Full CIP entry available.

Cover design, Section Heads, & "Domain" treatment: November Garcia
Cover illustrations: Tom Stolmar
Interior design: Heimat House
Author photo: Courtesy of Fotobooth, Shortlands, Kent, U.K.

Represented in Canada by Publishers Group Canada.

Distributed in Canada by PGC/Raincoast and in the U.S. by Small Press Distribution (SPD).

The publisher gratefully acknowledges the financial assistance of the Canada Council for the Arts, the Canada Book Fund, and the Province of British Columbia through the B.C. Arts Council and the Book Publishing Tax Credit.

Anvil Press Publishers Inc.
P.O. Box 3008, Main Post Office
Vancouver, B.C. V6B 3X5 Canada
www.anvilpress.com

PRINTED IN CANADA

. . . EATING SONGS, DRESSING SONGS, BATHING SONGS,
EVERYTHING. HE CAN'T DO ANYTHING UNLESS HE
MAKES IT A SONG.

— Mrs. P.

THE CONCRETE IS READILY IMBUED WITH FEELING
AND MEANING—MORE READILY, PERHAPS, THAN ANY
ABSTRACT CONCEPTION.

— Oliver Sacks

TO WALK AMONG PEOPLE
WITH THE OPEN SECRET OF BEING ALIVE.

— Octavio Paz

in memory of my father and mother

and for Colette

CONTENTS

THE ETERNAL PRESENT

MEMO TO WORDSWORTH

Hey Bill, the clouds don't look
so lonely from up here!
I'm wandering regardless,
passport strapped to thigh,
getting & spending frequent flier miles.
They call it globalization,
a mouthful-of-marbles mantra.
Daily, nightly, I sleep with the radio on.
What would you know from mantras,
deep as little Lucy up in Grasmere?
We shuffled past your comb at Rydal Mount.

Props for your daffodil mood swing,
the cloud-capped moors, the intimations.
I wonder too! My friends are difficult.
We tape ourselves, to know at last,
around those hand-turned oaken tables,
what you were talking so endlessly *about*,
hanging on your own every word.
Five summers! Tintern Abbey! River, flow!
Is it dead near Abbey Road down Penny Lane?
Can't find either on my plastic map
through sheets of English rain.

Say hi to Sam & Dorothy & the gang
(big hug to the missus) from the bloody future,
Age of Reasons branch, Eternally & Son,
parent to America Unchained.

Brother, you don't want to know.

IN MEMORY OF MYSELF

I.

Renovate me like one of your Victorians, San Francisco—

deck me out in color-coordinated sashwork & trim
 & plunk me down beside a looker
                              on a Sunday cable car

            from the turnaround at Woolworth's
alongside Union Square
                        all the way to the top of Russian Hill—

        (worlds away from the lunatic on Muni, picking nits
              off his matted hair to swallow: postcard that)

Allow my vagrant musings one more passage

            Cornerstoned in your Pyramid, O Pharaoh,
                  encrucibled, that I remain, rent-free,
                                    one last little present
from the Burton-Brown Machine
                    to its long receiving line of outstretched hands...

Tho I can no longer afford to pay the piper
                  even unto Turk off Jones
                              (the Haight long since a me-free zone),

Master Shorenstein, deport me not to Hayward—

            Bring the trust fund babies on,
                  the summer rain of CEOs,
                        day traders! catamarans! didgeridoos!

Let the future bury the future bury the future,
            until the risen Emperor Norton's ghost proclaims
        what went down between Mayor George & Super Dan
    a distant convoluted white man's quarrel

For today, bring me the head of Laffing Sal!

            Is this where Playland was?
                    & that was Sutro Baths, that unwashed fog?

        There we are, naked, stoned, at U.N. Plaza, in the fountain!

II.

O when will you embrace your blinking nipples, San Francisco—
        tho they tear the rose from her brow
            on the Starlight Room dance floor for all to see?

                    I know I am but an eyesore,
    to flatten to replace,
                short work for the wrecking ball, a hole
    to fill,
            to subdivide—
                    a sty of summer chills, mid-winter sweat

        & now now now now now, a broken record . . .

Renovate me, sub-basement to inscrutable scrollwork,
        Saint Francis & Sons, LLC—
            so I can bring at least a decent tax.

Rewire me to code & hit the switch!

To Left Coast digitized perfection,
                    rehabilitate my cool gray view!

Retrain your jazzbos to blow spread sheet,
                    wail those Floppy Disk Blues!

                              Hod carriers of keystroke,
stevedores,
               downloading bills of lading,
               downloading bills of lading,

          dragooned into the servitude of Boolean witchcraft!

          Bug eyes are the bay windows of the soul!

               Everywhere I go something beeps—

(LEAVENWORTH ST. BY DUSK)

Hey sexy, she says

Okay, she's a whore
still it's nice to hear

(The nature of my hunger, though,
lies elsewhere)

Half a block later
Joe Buck tips his hat

(Elsewhere still)

Hey Hey O.G.

(A brother at the corner
of Rise & Fall)

Sweated steamed lathered
toweled & groomed

at the Y,
I pilot two painted-on feet

meter to sick tree to meter,
by the steady stream

of floating red taillights
drawn along

ever so slightly uphill
through delicate charcoal degrees

of sky against which
a drunk in a doorway is dancing

as a woman instructs a small boy
This isn't the right place to cry

In the din lost almost forever,
a couple exchange their vows:

–Fuck You

–That's all you ever say—
You just say it, you don't do it

Wingless Night, enshroud our exhibitions

Hasten, tarry

UPON READING ABOUT FRANK LLOYD WRIGHT IN A RENTED BASEMENT ROOM

Granted, he was stranger than the lot of us.
I walked his dizzy plank once in Manhattan.

Tell me now can I find peace here underneath
This crazy quilt of pipe and restful waste,
Not giving a tinker's dam for a skyline view,
Designing my dream house one fever-night at a time?

SELF-PORTRAIT IN WORKFACE

First day no rain
all year, that's me,
shaking a pissgold rack

on Market Street
for the amusement
of whoever needs a laugh.

The sky, a pan
of grease, in city-states, ho, ho.
Peek-a-boo, Mr. Sun, you old letch!

(Pretty ones unsheathe,
a public offering, dream shares
of common flesh.)

Safe and soundless on page A2,
patient stats disclose:
HYPERTENSION, STROKES ON RISE

as January 18th in all its vainglory
feeds me whole to the meter of morning—
one thin dime of consciousness

putting on a madman's show,
sucked under, newspaperless.
"Relax," a street sage says, "it's only lies."

PROPHET LOSS STATEMENT

He was just here working the crowd, dispensing predictions,
and now like a set of keys—nowhere, in neither pocket,
gone. Don't call Missing Persons; not this time. Maybe he
got tired of our future perfect tense. Like our teams, the cor-
porate flagships, the postgrad nightlife yo-yo-yo's and every
three-piece that got signed with tour support.

No blame. A prophet has to eat, and he'd better sock some-
thing away. There isn't much as sad as yesterday's A-list oracle
pimping divination tapes on cable. An Eleusinian riddle this
is not.

As for us, this slump can't last, and he's not the only crystal
ball with legs. Next time, we'll throw a parade, steam clean
Union Square, sing like the sun and like we mean it.
Present—*nay*, bestow—a fortune cookie with the key to the
City inside. Keep on smiling!

The headquarters, the ball teams, the wheat beer drinkers,
they'll be back, and the bands after they get dropped. I can
feel it in all five of my metatarsal bones.

PAGES FROM A COURTING CHRONICLE

Someday I'm Gonna Make Her Mine

"The Beatles weren't," she holds,
luscious, menstrual, English,
Sunday morning in her bed, Let It Be
on a cassette in the boom box.
Though they broke up before she was born
in the Midlands in '73,
and the Pixies got her through school,
she came around.
"Ringo might be," I counter,
"don't forget the nose."
"Men are getting shorter,"
that one came last night,
and "I am *too* taller than you
in heels, my nose is higher than yours,"
as we stood there in the club.
Maybe we *are* getting shorter.
Maybe none of the Beatles were.
I draw myself up to my full horizontal height,
grazing softly somewhere soft.
"Leave Ringo alone," she says,
and I do.

The Gift

Some thing about a ring,
a dispute

over manners and romance,
who pays, and how,

and a lie about throwing it away,
a hurtful, needful lie

powder-packed with retribution
for breach by fiat suffered

at your mean, mean morning-mood hands.
The ring is safe—

not gold but silver,
in keeping with your wishes.

GHAZAL OF THE TERRIBLE TWENTIES

The fish store's a vid shoppe, bus stop still bus stop.
Bust a rhyme in 4/4 time and clean your fashion plate.

My self absorbing all that was never to be mine
from those stink-pretty pages. I who was never to be anyone's.

Something in the water, someday in the air, search engine
for your sampled thoughts, somewhere over . . . the radio.

Goth Almighty, Big Heart City—don't show your frosted mug
before 12:30, even if you *do* know the DJ's brother.

Robbed at gunpoint, 2 a.m., 19th & Valencia, for real.
They be trippin' on death juice, metal mouth, at large.

Next stop, Morning Breath. Monday rears its Medusa head.
Wet Food, Wet Food, Wet Food Now! Do *not* come home without it.

GHAZAL OF THE SUGARLESS GUMSHOE

The office bottle was dry, so I bought myself a vowel,
Once upon a girl whose fortune was her face.

Beneficiaries are good for business, take a seat.
She was blonde in the blue bleeding night, everywhere.

The gate rolls right. Missing necklace, slim chauffeur.
Something smells funnier than Buddy Hackett's act.

A city councilman goes for *how* much these days?
"You read too much, Einstein." Snap-brim *is* as snap-brim *does*.

Perish the thought—it died of old age, on my lips.
That lightly-dusted gauze runway, the sky, wept.

I took a left, another left, a short right, a hard left,
Then folded like a piece of linen, thinking *hey, no stars* . . .

NORTHERN CALIFORNIA DREAMING

It's a good day to have all this—
a promised land to zip around in,
a cruel tipsy blonde by my side,
the heat turned to high and gloves
of polished leather.
                              We park
to pop out like jacks-in-the-box,
to survey our immediate surroundings.
Are they not to our liking?
                                    Well then
we shall stuff ourselves back
in our coiled cube and be gone.
                                        There are
ever so many elsewheres on a day like today
with a snap in the air and no sun to dry
the tomatoes.
                    The end of the year
is inside us again. Our very bones
begin to worry: the parties!

THE REELECTION OF GOD (1999)

San Francisco.
Christmas Day.
Not a cloud
in the deep blue sky,
no wise men on display.
Not a shred of fleece
to blow away.

The Millennium
cries quits with us.
Every child,
every crossing guard,
an entrepreneur.
Will the chain letter
be unbroken?

The pollster asked
Does God exist?
71 percent of us
said *Yes.* And this
is a democracy
and that, friends, is
a landslide.

OLIVER OTHELLO KING, JR.

Take one divisive war. Add an inconvenient relic.
Bake until crisp. Air cool the rest of his life.

The name itself was worth five bucks. He shuffled up, a subter-
ranean shambles, past an activist gathering signatures: resolved, use
of marijuana be allowed for medicinal purposes. We were waiting
on the Civic Center outbound, most of us, heading home. "Hemp.
Been smoking it since '63." Standard issue bible beard and bedroll.
Been-there done-that pale blue eyes. "Two years in Nam. Just so
you can stand here. And I can't even get on the bus." He takes out
a wallet, extracts a driver's license, Glendale Federal, V.A., Social
Security cards—the latter soiled paper. "Quite a name, my friend."
"Double O King, that's what they call me." The N. We squeeze on.
"Airborne Rangers, Fort Campbell, Kentucky. How many people
you suppose you can kill in two years?" He says he's 53. HIV posi-
tive. T-cell count of 345. "They won't give me any money till I get
to 200." Has no idea how he got named. "He was a Moor. Wife ran
off and he killed her and a lot of other people. Only it wasn't his
fault." Been here since '75. Went to Alaska a couple times. Always
comes back to S.F., "like a homing pigeon." How he got sick:
"Heroin or hookers. Maybe both. I like drugs and women, so help
me God." We come out of the East Portal tunnel, into sudden dark-
ness, into pools of misted brilliant light. Brakes play their
high-pitched solo as I press the fin onto his palm. He draws himself
together, gives a comical salute, then strikes a ruined hero's pose,
his *coup de grace*. "Airborne Rangers. Death from the sky. Just so
you can stand here. All the way from Nam to Ocean Beach."

THE NEW LIBRARY

The New Library stands on the bones of the old.
In it are collected dross and diamonds,
Zane Grey to *Gray's Anatomy* on laser disc.
Gone, the dingy stairwells pooled with shadows
where castaways submerged their ruined eyes
adrift in *Das Glasperlenspiel.*

Light floods No One's Ark this time around.
Corkscrew steps high, wide and handsome
outspin Fred and Ginger, eating bookshelf feet.
The cornerstone projected in 3-D.
The Children's Place, the donor's brand.
The Mayor's Liaison, who gives himself a hand.

Online in his sanctum sanctorum,
Chief Librarian Bleep plays cards,
then photoshops Gutenberg's head
onto a football sailing over a goalpost.
Nicholson of Berkeley, ink-stained Tribune
of the Past, issues jeremiads from the basement.

Waving a yellow notepad full of crime,
dog-staunch Bilarius eggs his hero on.
They sleuth, they smart, they strap
themselves to a card catalogue.
Soon no one will remember what one is.
(Dewey lives to fight another day.)

Overstock too old to adopt is 'taken away'.
"BROWN SHIRTS IN PIXEL CLOTHING!" shrieks Bilarius,
unheeded, a martyr, a fool...
Contemplation—now *that's* a dead issue,
what with all the schools of literature
letting out at once.

WITH COLETTE AT THE EDINBURGH CASTLE

Outshining Christmas at Macy's,
    English rose with a French coquette's name,
        she turns heads from red heels to her Wreck of the Hesperus
        hair as we enter the fray—
            pulsing dim loud speaker hiss
                darts   pool a phone booth in back
                    trivia game Eighties Night mid-question:

. . . *PLAYED THE SON, BUT WHO PLAYED THE FATHER?*

        Memory lane for beginners.

She had her Chimay before dinner,
absinthe after, over ice in a flute.
                        Again?
A splash. Me of course tragically sober,
here to cut loose with a pint.
Friday after dark. We slide in.
Sticky table, slow service,
pizza breath in the air,

        cut with

a sight for sore vinegar eyes:
Fish & Chips in newsprint.
Olde Chelsea on Larkin delivers.

They don't build joints like this anymore, they pull them down.

Behind me, in a booth, a tribe her own age
is having too good a time.
                    Her VOICE!

right through my spine! Colette shouts
across the table, at my ear. I say something
back. Did she hear?
                           She leans in, standing up,
grabs my face and plants a kiss, in front of everyone,
in bar light, approaching full bloom.

Game over   put your pencil   in the cup.

One more round. Brown and sweet. We touch glass,
we touch wood, hearts in Highlands, halfway home.

HAT HAIR

I have hat hair
and friends I never see,

walking up Cole to 17th,
heading where I don't want to go,

undaunted by oncoming foot traffic,
scratching sounds on a missing pet flyer,

a card-carrying anybody
nine lines out of ten,

with no daughter to spoil, to disappoint,
no son to blame-forgive, blame-forgive,

no team to follow,
all my hair, all my teeth,

my subpar digestive function—
that's me

alright already,
dashing as a dunce cap,

cat lover not dog fighter,
86'd at the favor bank,

Saint Selfish at your service,
dragging my dad into this.

Look, there I am!
flossing like faith incarnate,

cooped up inside this poem
with all that sun outside.

CURIOUS SONG

Who are these people
  Dressed all in black
Where are they going
  Outstripping the dark

Did they ever lie down
  To weep without reason
Do they come in pairs
  Is Haight Street their Ark

Did they ever wear yellow
  Tell me—did they
Yellow down to the ground
  All at once, look away

Does something signal
  Urging them on
Will birds be waiting
  Red ones or blue

Are they secretly happy
  Dressed all in black
Behind their sunglasses
  Can I go too

WASHINGTON, D.C., 1863

Pen in hand, Walt Whitman
(*I loafe* et cetera) waited for him
to pass, with his *latent sadness...*
deep-cut lines... grave appellation,
astride *an easy-going gray horse,*
surrounded by a company of cavalry
in their *yellow-striped jackets, sabres drawn.*

Or he came *in an open barouche,*
to his right a young boy on a pony,
always the same dusky lieutenant
in charge of the men, aglint.

Early summer, his odd wife
in complete black, with a long crape veil
accompanied him *on a pleasure ride*
through the capital at dawn, drawn on
only by two horses, nothing extra.

Walt Whitman, now a regular sight
(*I loiter, sing, assume*), they took to exchanges
of bows, of nods, *and very cordial ones,*
each to his station (a wise hat knows its head),
as the blood tide slowly turned in the War Between the States.

The President would later assist him
to gain a clerk's post, second class
in the Indian Bureau. The affair was that one-sided.

◎   ◎   ◎

Walt Whitman, having the time
(see him *loiter, loafe,* sop a fevered brow)
inhaled the lilac's strong perfume
as a thrush sang death, sang beauty, all night long.
Tomorrow, he would attend to the wounded again.

In a *spell of fine soft weather,* he admired
the moon, and *the President's house,* pen in hand.

THE WORLD STAGE
(an exit)

As in a dream he will touch down
On the tarmac of his homeland
Wave to the crowd one more time
(The transplant did not 'take')
A king is flying east to die

He has spent half a life above these clouds
Casting his nation-length shadow
With no oil fields to keep friends at bay
Not for him the assassin's bullet
Nor the backstairs palace ballet

Already she is in mourning
His blue-eyed fairy-tale queen
Standing vigil as he stood by her—
Revered, respected, hated or beloved
A king lies on a gurney in the sky

This world, he knows better than most,
Must soon unravel at the seams
His people divided, pent-up
His neighbors redrawing their maps
The little fellow has become a man of peace

They will bury him in style
Then behind the scenes, watch out
For now, though, he's alive
Awake, still in command
A king asks for a glass of water

DYSFUNCTIONAL DON

The cement shoes was a cry for help
says his nephew Sam "The Namesake"
in his drugstore paperback.
Capo of Chicago, failed assassin
of Fidel, freelance CIA consultant,
he died a cornered sphinx
on his way to testify—
a cheap-moral end to a make-the-rules ride,
plastered in the dailies 48 points high:
SUGAR DADDY TO PRESIDENT'S DOLL
BLOWN AWAY BY HIS OWN BOYS
"The Namesake" humps his book on an AM
talk show, says how it felt to wear that name
in classrooms, on résumés.
From Portland to Dubuque
first-time callers clear their throats
to rehearse their long hellos.
Uncle Sam's abused upbringing. Made him
a distant father. With acute low self-esteem.
A vicious homophobe.
All the protection money, the gallons of fear and respect,
couldn't buy an ounce of closure,
an approving look from *his* old man.
He never could locate the source of his anger,
or sit through a song by Sinatra.

THE LOVE BUS

"I thought I was marrying a female Johnny Rotten.
Instead, I got this right-wing Phyllis Diller."
                                    —first husband James Moreland

Courtney Love herself they say
used to ride these very workhorse Geary buses,
smacked back to the gills,
nasty to look at and full of spit & snarl.
Girlfriend wasn't shit.
That's how it happens when it does—
yesterday's skank is tomorrow's
Grammy nominee, yellow ribbon and all
in a loaned-out designer dress
nobody will dare ask her to return.
Yeah, well, she sure stunk up the joint around here
long before Adam Duritz stopped washing his hair.

Oh the stories these bus routes could tell!
The poor shlumps lurching home with work-dead faces
and Here She Comes, a human hypodermic syringe
wishboning out of a pair of Doc Martens,
hellbent to show this whole burnt-out town
that next to her Janis was a faggot
and a no-talent punk daddy's girl
waiting around for some sucker
to put a rock on her finger and slap her into line.

THE BARBER OF HAIGHT ST.

Mr. Sampas had a pole outside
and not much of his own,
and I always got sent back.
Mitzi had volumes, and magic fingers,
and was available but not to me.
Jerry's whereabouts are unresolved.
He moved from Gil's shop to his house
to a p.o. box to a message phone.
Last time I saw him, on public transit,
he was a haunted skeleton
who took my 'loan' and address, mumbling.

What with the discontinuities
the one-time-only faces
a barber is an anchor
somewhere to return from.
As I keep getting up, from different chairs.

Kelly is my current secret sharer,
a strapping milk-fed queen
who left Green Bay
"two minutes after high school."

Now he's the Sculptor of the Lower Fillmore Head Shot.
Who never looks remotely like he did the time before.

Waiting for him to show,
10:00 a.m., Saturday morning,
surrounded by spiked heels, hair wraps
and ambient Euro-noise,
I have never felt less fabulous.

(They can also serve your eyebrow
arching needs, rebalance dreads,
through purple beaded curtains in the back.)

I catch up on smack
about the Hollywood Madam,
then wade into my black on green
SELECTED POEMS OF EDWIN ARLINGTON ROBINSON
MORTON DAUWEN ZABEL, EDITOR, INTRODUCTION BY JAMES DICKEY.
Kelly doesn't ask what I'm reading anymore.
He calls in—he's getting up, he's on his way.

WORKS AND DAYS

FOR THE SAN FRANCISCO CHRONICLE'S QUESTION MAN

Same jokes for eighteen years, six times a week.
You weren't a man at all. "A wind-blown blonde

with emerald isle eyes," you put strangers
instantly at ease, five per column, "armed

with a point-and-shoot and pad and ready smile."
Bad days "like pulling taffy," yeoman's work

on a corner, in a square or by a fountain.
People stood around to hear you ask:

1964: *Should wives have an allowance?*
1971: *Are you wearing a toupee?*

1981: *Do your parents know you're gay?*
1982: *Who's the worst driver you know?*

(I can't not ask one back to you. Stay mum
or signal as you please: *Is this our only life?*)

Bone Cootes fingered me as the worst driver,
to your third successor, who recycled.

The column disappeared, a curio.
Mouse clicks were the hound on newsprint's trail.

Today, still winter elsewhere, sun and birdsong, an obit—
one lifetime shrunk-to-fit, a pocket world:

The very cadence of your name—Novella O'Hara.
Your "bootlegger parents" must've been merry that day!

In your youth you "toured Army bases in North Africa"
performing in "a three-woman troupe."

Harry Jupiter recalls the way you danced
"so slow, so close—but only with her husband!"

FOR LAUGHS

Dick Shawn, a name in his day,
pure energy poured into flesh,
legend while he lasted, didn't.
No one do. He filled the hall
that night at UC San Diego:
kids mostly, and some profs
with ponytails and co-ed dates,
fat cats and wise gray chicks
who'd seen him slay the Hungry I in '56.
And one of his own children. A new bit,
about his heart attack, for laughs—
and laugh it up they did,
wave on wave of joyride sound
as he lay there working the room
to beat the band, fibrillating
now for real, ventricular,
reliving his panic, dying in public,
horizontal, center stage, is there a doctor in the house?

WILD WILD WAYS

Don't mention the old days.
You're talking to yourself again.

Somewhere between the bar and the café
you got lost at sea and drowned
in your tears on the sunken dance floor
in the spinning light the storm-watch night,
as the band went overboard, over a face
that is the absolute harbor of desire,
featureless, irresistible,
end of song.

You're talking to the girl you used to be.
Saying what you needed to hear.

LESTER ROGERS

"I did a stupid thing" & he did,
the kind that draws a crowd of uniforms,
drawn guns, a swarm of wide-brimmed funny hats.
"The pay-off was too fat to resist.
Drive a load of herb to Massachusetts,
too easy to call work," says Lester Rogers,
silver-headed, silver-bearded Rocky Mountain buccaneer,
forty-two years of faded jeans & one long river,
breaking silence to a stranger on a train.
He rubs in Tiger Balm & pours out
an after-dinner shot of Jagermeister,
on his way to be arraigned, rolling east,
blue-black windows pressing in on either side.
(He offers me a shot, retakes the footlight.)
"Pulled me over outside Davenport
for Colorado plates. Cited me. Not wearing a seatbelt."
The police dog made a beeline for the "dog-proof" plastic bags.
"So much for too easy to call work.
Should've known, I never won a gamble in my life.
Even if I'd wanted to, who would I give up?
Never knew any names or saw their faces—
the arrangements were all made with codes & pagers."
Carpet-layer by weekday, musician by most nights—
zydeco, country rock, bluegrass, novelty—
up-at-dawn, straight-wages, trout-fishing Lester
got popped, in God's country with a cargo of good shit.
"Better Iowa than Illinois," he shrugs.
A lawyer flew his own plane in from Tucson,
posted Lester's bail on his own bond.

Now Lester must keep his appointment—
"Mexico? Yeah, right. I have a daughter—"
probation, deferred sentence, heavy fine,
or stand forth & pray for strength to do his time.
He pours another shot on his way to do just that.

THE ALPHA BETA MALE

He dusts and does windows
comparison shops
can bake a cherry pie
served warm right from the sill

His whites are white
His colors sing opera

In his daydreams a jewel thief of hearts . . .

Dinner on the table promptly or else
And a piquant aroma it is
Smell those bay leaves
Cover and simmer
Arrowroot thickens the sauce
A mad dash of Parmesan
Voila!

Dates glance sidelong in vain
for signs of disarray
and leave early, feeling
outflanked? redundant? what?

While he was out his mother did not call

Like a sand dab surfing the Discovery Channel
he follows the stock market tides
all the while scratching at
his existential itch

Without surgery or prosthesis,
loin of his fragrant loins,
coupon clipper, redeemer extraordinaire—
he has become his own Little Woman

Hardbound books on either side of a double bed:

The Courage To Be Intimate
Shoot The Wounded, Hold The Guilt

THE ATTORNEY ARRIVES AT HIS OFFICE
ON APRIL 16th

Of course it would be dark,
the accounting firm next door,
on the ultimate day after the night before.
People hate lawyers and pity the bean counter.
People hate themselves and withhold pity from the poor.
Across my desk not one of you
can look me in the eye.
Straight-faced, I hear your flimsy alibi.
Take next door your shoebox of receipts.

You want miracles, try Lourdes.
No more can my dog play Hot Cross Buns
than a CPA scramble the code
and make pearls from a string of sham zeroes.
Mob fantasy stuff. The movies.
They eat alone at their desks,
rub their temples same as me.
We sell our eyesight by the hour.
In pursuit of the rock bottom line.

Are the crunchers at home sleeping in?
Up at dawn shredding wheat at loose ends?
Did they traipse off to Palm Springs together?
The way dollar signs pass through their hands
like a rope trick, you'd never
know from the burn marks on mine.
Do they tally each provident thrust?
As for me, I plead out every case.

Today may as well be tomorrow—
on anybody's sabbath more laws than hearts get broken.
Enough get caught to keep me late tonight.

SLAB OF CONSCIOUSNESS

The girl in the black dress. The cabbie. Midnight. He did it. Kissed her. Killed her. Or did not. Whereabouts. The cops. The press. The D.A. Statements, gaps, denials. Albert. At the Flame. Olympic Flame. Pissing Hedy off. Saying rush to judgment. Saying wait. The facts. It's gone: Her future. Bright. The town. On it. At the Bubble Lounge. Outside. A fare like any other. Dumped. The body. Him. Her ATM. Caught on tape. Page one. Her photograph. Blonde. Pretty. His. Muslim. Swarthy. Grim. Off. Cut 'em, both, Hedy says. Albert shrugs. A refill? Not a chance. Results. Still inconclusive. Weeks away. Semen. And if so? His lawyer says: *con-sen-su-al*. Breathing. She stopped breathing. People do. Husband. Father of two daughters. Record, none. Party girl. Hard stuff. Her friends: No way. Ahead. Of her. Whole life. And him? Paths crossed. The rest. Her service. Beautiful. An overflow. A year from now: his trial. Jurors. Experts. Shrinks. The Bubble Lounge. Too much to. Wandered off. Midnight. The cabbie. The girl in the black dress.

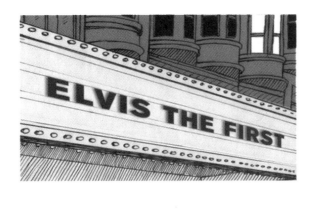

ELVIS THE FIRST

> A father is a monarch.
> No one elected him.
>   —Erich Adler

I.

It was the Summer of '68,
the Summer of Love somewhere.
Turn and cough, my father told him
in the Spanish-style villa,
say ahhh, and looked within
the castle keep, the throat
that sang "Heartbreak Hotel."

He pierced the royal flesh, that much we know,
and then Dad stuck it to them, every one,
inside the walled compound, the King's
men all lined up for B12 shots.

Dad was no Doc Feelgood.
Cholesterol, the Silent Killer,
He tried to warn the King.
A matter of a pound-a-day cheddar cheese habit.

Elvis watched cartoons
those housecall Saturday mornings,
off the patio, a stranger to the sun.
Top Cat, a lesser Felix.
Till I was nine I watched it myself.

Would I like to come along
three times he had to ask
before I found a hole in my schedule.
Dylan was my God, no Jesus-slop for him.

I reclined among the shadows, bored,
giraffe-neck-skinny trees, an oblong pool—
a pool's a pool and palm trees
lined Palm Canyon Drive.

Colonel Tom paced the perimeter,
mapping out the Reconquest of Vegas.

Tall and fit and thin.
Typing paper-pale, ridiculously handsome.

Marked absent from this page.
Try. Call him. Concentrate...

Pleased t'meet ya, klip.

(The three of us, and this
my only camera.)

I stammered something back,
and we were in dad's bag-brown '65 Polara, heading home.

II.

HE DROVE A TRUCK AND CUT A COUPLE SIDES
DID LIP CURLS THROUGH A THOUSAND MIDNIGHT RIDES

FLEW ACROSS THE CONTINENT FOR SNACKS
GAVE CADILLACS AWAY LIKE LUNCH, HELD PLAQUES

SEQUINS YE SHALL FIND, THE STAGE A SNARE
HIS HEART SHUT DOWN AND NOW HE'S EVERYWHERE

III.

I tried and failed to tell myself that story. Mom serving Rock
Cornish game hen, mash potatoes with skim milk, mar-
garine (no sour cream), steamed broccoli, head and stalk.
Iced tea or lemonade (no sugar). Ice milk for dessert. At the
old house, on Morongo Road. And where he sat. The guy
sleeping in the limousine outside. Mom felt sorry for him,
that much I remember, he and his pretty wife had broken
up. Did he notice there wasn't a stereo in our living room?
(They didn't listen to music anymore, after Dad put his reel-
to-reel Magnavox away. He'd played it through the speakers
by the pool, hooked up by Harry Cosmos who built the
place. Jolson or the Mills Brothers, splashed with pastel light,
in that oleander-ringed backyard.) Did I say it never hap-
pened, that they fought? She lost. Would the King have
come? Not likely. Then again, with everything undone, the
epic boredom, flat-out weirdness on the airwaves . . . He
must have sat through some tough ones with Priscilla and
her family. Ours had few social graces, and we knew noth-
ing about the South. My oldest brother would have been
reading Baudelaire. My sister, I guess, was okay. I bet he
would have ma'am'd Mom to death.

IV.

(Dance Mix)

Walk! Walk! Walk! shouted Dad a la Kathryn Kuhlman
He's just frightened, said Mom, meaning us both
Then they sent me to the bone man, Dr. Baldwin—
mallets x-rays blood work questions crutches
(Then) (our hands) (shook) (by the pool)
(outside the Spanish-style villa) (sliding glass)
The next day I woke up and I could walk!
That's the part I keep skipping, okay . . .
Now I'm going to work right here
bleeding all over the page
is my stage and I shall not not want
for the Lord is my Home Shopping Network.
Reclining shadows bored neck skinny trees
outside the Spanish-style villa
inside the walled compound
where he touched me, two years still
till my first joint (Summer of Love but where?)
It wouldn't take my weight. My leg.
Left leg. Left hip. Crutch-Crutch.
Then (handshake) (crutches) (sliding glass)
(the pool) (giraffe neck trees) Did I walk? I did! I walked!
All over the page is my stage. Long Live the King!
The Brits had knocked him stiff, BAM! BIFF!
a Fillmore Cocktail chaser (Somewhere, Love)
(Spanish-style villa) (B12 shots)
Might as well be shots of water
Dad stuck it to them, Mom
(no sour cream) (stalks) (lemonade).
I tried. The King held plaques,
gave Cadillacs, drove trucks everywhere

Morongo Road. Outside. The limo guy.
Mom felt bad for Henry Miller too!
Look Ma, no crutches! Better? All.
Rick went to Reed, dropped out, came home, came home—
running from the rabbi's house (crib, lair)
screaming *Cut my balls off! Cut them off!*
Rick and his beanpole friend Mark Bishop
crashed a Panther (Black) meeting in blackface
in Portland high on acid
too hypomanic to lay a beating on.
Then Dad got snubbed in Vegas
(tickets, show, mix-up)
and sent the King his royal records back
(pre-sliced) (pound-a-day) (the Silent Killer)
And now I'm bleedingbleeding
bleeding all over the page is my cage and I shall not
not put the Lord in my cart at HomeShoppingNetwork.com
Jolson and the Mills Brothers, look look, no Ma!
Afterward, the condition that could never be
properly diagnosed disappeared as
they lined up, they kept lining up

FANFARE

*Space
begat
Time
begat
Sky
begat
Sea*

*Matter
begat
Matter
begat
Life*

*The
Congress
of
These States
begat
the Presidency*

*Robert
Michael
Lipschutz
took a Wife*

They Liked Ike

He teed off
straight & clean as sun is light

making peace
as natural as war

(the dirt about his driver
saved for later)

yonder caddy sweating buckets
full of shade

True & tall as grass is green
he thundered "*FORE!*"

Beware the Military-Industrial Complex"
(Cassandra never had a harder sell)

On the back nine
I befell

Jewish parents of Republican persuasion
not yet retired Democrats

A bear in a mansuit came to visit
carrying his own cheap clubs

& pounded his heavy shoe right on the table!

The Brothers K

A dynasty that never was . . .
"They shot them boys like state fair ducks,"
I think I read somewhere.

Nᵢₖₜₐ **L**ₒᵥₑₛ **F**ᵢₑₗ **!**
JFK himself
wrote on the toilet wall of Air Force One,
a tenured professor told me in a bar.

◎   ◎   ◎

Hot pearls of pain ran down his overmedicated spine,
as Marilyn made love to "Happy Birthday."

Didn't they send us home early
from elementary school?

Didn't the other shoe drop?

I shaped the word with my small pink tongue:
ăss-ăss ăss-ăss ăss-ăss ăss-ăss ĭn-ā-shŭn

A word with a future in this company.

We Interrupt This President

My Fellow Americans said the Texan to the Country.
All the while his v.p. was pleased as punch.

Those were the schoolnights, gathered in the den. The couch.
Dad's feet. Uncle Walter. Three Networks under God.

71

They say he had major stick. He sure carried himself that way.
(The Cock Robin Commission embraced the lone sparrow theory.)

He was large in other ways, he married off his daughters.
Who knows just what he had on those sorry s.o.b.'s up on the Hill.

Come back when your teeth get out of jail said a girl.
We were six around the table where I never could sit still.

He inherited a war, it hung him out to dry.
All the cowboy boots in Corpus couldn't change a thing.

I Am Not A Haiku

The whole gang showed up
for the funeral, as if
under subpoena.

You The Man

Another Ford from Michigan
once coveted the White House.

Henry hated Jews as much as Hitler
hated Russia. Oh but Jerry

played the slow-wit to a fault,
handed off the ethnic jokes to others,

with a head like a helmet, two knees to replace,
and assumed the Oval Office in reverse.

[inset: grainy photograph: boy, goal post, dusk:
"East Grand Rapids High, doing wind sprints"]

Wanting It

with lust in my heart to see my name
spelt out in Mom's favorite magazine

Jimmy Carter sent his in to *The New Yorker*
exactly like anybody else,

and received a personal response,
unlike, say, you or me.

Why, he wrote back, is my verse
not up to what you print?

Stands to reason—if poets make peanuts . . .
(The editor endeavored to reply.)

Even Stalin, a touchier Georgian,
took a stab in his fumbling youth.

And an Emperor snuck from his box
to fight slaves in the Colosseum.

But those, the singer sang, were different times.
Examples go begging for love.

Maybe we should try the slams.
Or the American Treasury of Verse Contest.

TWO TURNS FOR THE GIPPER

No Sweat

All the rage, it was, to say:
"I'm leaving the country if *he* gets elected."

See ya!

(We are all categorically, constantly, coming and going.)

Veni, vidi, vici, Manny, Moe & Jack,
he took a bullet for Jodie and gave it right back.
Climbed the polls like a rodeo clown!

So he never played Hamlet.
So his wife was the worst.

So he gave us nuclear nightmares
as the Communist Threat deconstructed,
as the debt went platinum, twice.

What ever.

No, I didn't—share in the prosperity.
My best friend overdosed on alcohol and
died never having witnessed a computer.

I sought asylum in San Francisco.

NURSERY RON

With nary a wink or a nod
He denied that he dyed.

To make fires for Mommy and God
He swung the axe blade.

He denied that he'd lied
And continued to fade.

The Bunkport Chronicles (*reformatted to fit your screen*)

Kenny Bunkport took a spin / in his hungry boat around a thirsty lake

Took a jog on skinny legs Kenny did / then wandered off message some say

he ran contra & harried the missus / with scattershot dropping of bombs

The guests arrive at five so look alive / the distaff Bunkport fumed

Marshaling her not-so-secret plan / she wielded her registered weapon

I've a headcold in my gout / Dinner went down like a drug deal

till she put lots of compound between them / He dropped a smarter bomb—roses!

And it fell in his lap, his own war! / The sky failed to roast Chicken Little

despite Kenny's hapless precautions / He went back to both places he came from

Horndog Agonistes

He's back from Africa. He's back from China.
Issuing executive orders left and right.
Sixteen scandals later, bring it on.

He's on the magic horn to Gerry Adams.
Took Joe Camel to the shed and whaled away.
He's back from a long session in the john.

Where were you, Miss Marples the First Lady.
Issuing executive orders left and right.
Doing the job, the job, the job, the job.

Tornado in the Midwest, don't look now:
There he is, hand on some pain-pulsing shoulder,
Baptist sound bites honeying the air.

V-chips, warning labels, clouded water from the tap.
He's issuing executive orders left and right.
A chicken inspector in every other pot.

Meanwhile, Mister Ken scrubs his scrotum:
There was a bad man from Hope / Who dropped his Ivory soap . . .
Such powdered balls, Mister Ken—all for who?

Stroke of the pen. Law of the land. No lie.
He's issuing executive orders left and right,
to protect the black-white-brown-red-yellow toys.

Me, I don't care to know how they make sausage.
Twice unhitched, with broken parents and no car,
I can almost feel his big paw on my shoulder.

Interview With An Echo

Is there precedent for censuring the President?
There is no precedent for censuring the President.

Is there sentiment for pressuring the President?
There is sentiment.

Are there impediments?
Imps. Pediments.

Some are adamant?
Big time, big tent.

What about impeachment?
Snake pit? Am I It?

You're *It* alright, mothah, to your eyeholes. You'll wish
you'd bought the farm at Khe Sanh when we're through.
And your partner-in-sleaze Hilarious, take her with. All
hail the Gangster-of-Love-in-Chief! the Rail-Splitter-of-
Hairs! Pants-on-Fire! Hot enough?
No comet.

Sex?
Next.

Balance? Malice? Melons? Phallus? Felon? Humpty? Alice?
Checks.

Sit right down.
Daddy, let your mind roll on.

This Drawn And Quartered Moon

DECEMBER 2000

It hangs there like a broken toy
cut out, unpainted, crude

a toothless faceless grin
stationed over Tallahassee

the election given, Rehnquist's gift, outright...

(Mom's ashes in a turquoise vase
next to a table lamp—)

(Mario, my road dog, locked away
a hundred years—)

No it won't be setting soon
this drawn and quartered moon

DOMAIN

Every cigarillo
A barista's lazy eye
All the literary horses
Each head of hair on fire
HE IS ITS PRESIDENT TOO

Zsa Zsa, J.Lo, Uma
County parks in fifty states
His cousin Herb who voted Green
A put-to-sleep-cat's grieving widow, ditto
HE SOLEMNLY SWORE ON A STACK

Baseball teams he never owned
Lions and tigers and bears in a cage
Skull and Bones lock, stock and barrel
Painted deserts choked with shopping malls
HIM! AT THAT DESK! IN THAT CHAIR!

Bad blood spilt on poison fruit
More chads than you can count
Colonies of monarch butterflies
Darkness visible and Light obscured
YOU GROW INTO THE JOB, YOU GROW A PAIR

From God's mouth to his own jug ears
In sickness and in health and neither one

The Tooth Father, Naked at Last
after Robert Bly

The vice president has spoken
from an undisclosed location

in immaculate Pig Latin
as a favor to the nation.

WE INTERRUPT THIS PROGRAM:
He reverts to grade school English,

sees a pussy, purrs *Nice doggie*,
while playing with his dingus,

and pointing at the sun
thunders *Moon* then bellows *Mine*.

He downs a beer, he smacks his lips,
pronounces it *Good wine*.

The Trial of ███████ ██ ███ — *a fantasia*

Several raps of Her Honor's tri-colored dildo bring the Court to
order. Rulings may arise on short notice, ergo she maintains her grip.

The gallery is packed with daytime tv talk show fans. ALL RISE.

A dreamy look in progress on his mug, the Assistant U.S. Attorney
cracks his knuckles then pops a hard-on pill. You never know when
that sardonic sloe-eyed bailiff might call an impromptu side bar.

The defender sports a bow tie and a cowlick a la Dagwood. His client has not shown—hey, it works for Lindsay Lohan, why not for The ███████ in ████? Besides, the Court's reach is still shy of its grasp (a protracted pissing match over venue).

When █ ██ ███ was found guilty, also in absentia, his expensive new best friend, his lawyer, was appointed as his proxy "for all purposes arising from these proceedings." The parties went to chambers and the counselor made egress on a gurney, only technically alive.

Ergo, Mr. Bow Tie, Appearing For Incurious ██████, does not check his messages or watch; he bounces on his toes, hypervigilant, wide eyes up front, sweating like a pig.

Futures (October 29, 2008)

"Snow globes shake like castanets."
Nostradamus said it better, said it first.
In my recurring nightmare we're immersed.

The deck is marked? Since always. I'm all in.
One share, one vote, one wild card to win.
Future futures go on sale next Tuesday.

Past pasts are blooded over. See you at 16th & Mission.
The grey hound plays old tricks for pole position,
Racing to the bottom of the age.

Our new and improved national nightmare needs a break

Gonna wash that first mate,
The whole slick crew, out of my hair
In driving rain off Ocean Beach, takeout fusion in the air.

The wind also blows—pods with worlds-to-be inside.
Past futures play the margins. What's a margin?
There's always dirt to turn up in my garden.

When I said I love you, did I cross a line?
Without a carapace, a loaded weapon or a sign,
You set my heart on fire when I saw you standing there.

Our new and improved national nightmare needs a break

MR. INSIDE CLEARS THE ROOM

Blood can't sing, and angels
won't tell you different.
Objects fall in love then out,
I've seen it with these gimlet eyes.
My trap is neither tender nor speedy.
Hand me a critical blind alley
and I'll give you back Interstate 5
wrapped in a ribbon like Christo.
Not much survives sandblasting,
or 24-7 surveillance. Anyone?
You remind me of a dancer,
who ate custard on a bun.
Settle down, my featherless
friend, if you know what's
good for the gander.

THE PLAGIARIST HONES HIS APOLOGIA

These very words are stolen to begin with.
From a cheap pocket dictionary. Ha!
No, I highjacked a Scrabble game
and rearranged the letters. Hee!
Not from anywhere exactly,
though *originally* . . . Hie!
Hold on there, ossifer—
once, maybe thrice,
all a misunder-
standoff. Ooh,
down where
her locks
curl. Do
Re Mi.
Feh!
So?

THE DISAPPOINTED CULTIST GETS A FEW THINGS OFF HIS CHEST

I was her #1 fan
I worshiped the paper
she typed on
the notes she hit and missed
the perfect word misplaced
Now something is gone—
somehow and slightly
the right touches add up to wrong.

Am I hearing what I'm saying?

I loved the pockmarks on her skin...
I was there at the beginning,
when she discovered herself
like a new world across
an interior ocean.
I saw her land, send out scouts,
set up colonies, conquer.

I'm sending myself into exile

THE TV WEATHERMAN RATS HIMSELF OUT

Why does the rain run off
and where does it go
in such an unladylike hurry?
And what about snow—

drifting as slow as a twelve-year-old boy
waking up.
(My four-year-old stepdaughter
feeds a doll drop by eye drop.)

Sunlight is silent
and gives me a chance to shine too.
It cures and it kills'
and feeds plants and has nothing to prove.

Okay, so my ad libs are scripted.
Like *you're* never wrong.
Try running a 10K in *my* teeth.
Go drown your lawn.

THE UNKNOWN LYRIST'S EASTER SUNDAY
SERMON TO HIMSELF

National Poetry Month or no,
I am, per usual, alone,
in that dreary little cul-de-sac
removed from luck and light,
BOOKS ON TAPE and MYSTERY,
green to yellow COOKING,
the bitter dream of TRAVEL,
surrounded by the pure pith of the ages,
the rotten, ripe and wax fruit of the age.
My eyes fall on an argument,
The Ordeal of Robert Frost,
no doubt misshelved, well-reasoned prose,
which I don't disturb,
having ordeals of my own.

Outside a weak sun shines
as my Rockports carry me
back to my Tendernob cavern.
(What used to be a "garret, carpet new"
now lists as "atmospheric, skyline view.")

Okay, he had it hard, we know, we know.
The hired hand comes home to die,
that much I recall, God-fearing solid souls
take him in. Apples, birches, fences,
the virtues of persistence and blank verse.
Still no matter how you slice it,
the ordeal of Robert Frost has gone to sleep.

I on the other hand rock on
from crisis to conceit,
elegy to chorus, cheek to cheek,
beset by editors and landlords without faces.

An early April afternoon could've gone worse.
One's bookworm cul-de-sac is the apple of another's universe.

GOING PUBLIC

Holy Guacamole! We wuz warned,

as we elbowed our sibs
in those putt-putt boats (six-seaters)

chasing the other famblies around
(mom & pop nucular famblies around)
around a fake lagoon

—at a nice safe uniform distance
—on (domestically manufactured) submersible tracks

                                        chased in turn
and serenaded
by a plague of mechanical
                    pests

pop-up helium voices reaching critical mass:

   "...IT'S A SMALL, SMALL WORLD."

         Warned with wax in our ears...

Just today I emailed another death threat to Malaysia,
and not 10 minutes later received a reply(!):

Comm and gut me, ashsole.

I wuz only kidding (he's my homey),
but those caroling castrati,
they meant business,
the graffiti on the wall deconstructed into global

            Market Share.

Mickey, you knew it too.
(Color-blind flags look alike in the wind.)

You always thought big
for a rodent.

Big period, come to think.
In the Magic Kingdom Polaroid,
you were taller than Dad!

Back then chips came in baskets
fried crisp (first one's free!)
and Carol Doda baked Silicone Valley
from scratch.

What the aitch-e-double-hockey-sticks did *we* know?

So sorry to hear about you and the missus.
That took real old-school class
when they blindsided you outside
Le Cirque du Fromage,

a bouquet of throbbing hand mics
straight out of Sigmund Freud
stuck in your trap:

"I wish Garfield and Minnie
no end of happiness."

          Not me.
            A vow is a vow.
               Even in California.

Some days you're the only America we have left.

ROUNDER

The bowling ball jumps his lane again, disrupting a dispute between the Brothers Grimm. He gives handles to the regulars. These two huff and puff, over every frame. The ceiling spins, the walls spin too, seen one gutter, seen them all . . .

He dreams about the way things used to be: when balls were black, like him, except the occasional swirl; fishnets and cigars; pinballs in motion; pencils; score sheets; high-pitched shrieks and whoops. Then he dreams he has long legs of polyurethane. When he comes to he is churning, inside a sea of foam, with a dent hard by his finger hole; after being heat-dried he makes his midnight rounds, knocking the remains of three pints awash in fruit flies off a tray. "Hey Red, you up?" His best friend is a bottle refilled ad nauseam, from a spout countersunk into big tin cans of ketchup. Late mornings are their favorite, when the alleys get a shine that fills the air.

Racked in for the night, he replays his Downward Spiral: open frames, splits under pressure, long weekends in unfamiliar bags. ("In the bag *and* in the bag," quips Red, "we should call you Double Down.") Marks from who knows where; a gouge that breaks the polisher. He feels like a boulder in a tux. Anymore, the game itself—"don't call it a *sport*"—can set him off. "I don't have a problem, you're my problem," he warns 2-Pin, to what passes for his face.

So he reins himself in, has a week without a blackout, even puts three spares together in a row; things are humming along until one afternoon, KABOOM: "They're forming a new league." It's Raylene. She answers call lights at a crawl, delivering the 411 to anyone who'll listen. "Software guys, with custom balls. They say ours are heavy, and they stick. We even still have one that has two holes."

◎　　◎　　◎

In the basement of the church assorted articles, appliances and tools sip-sip at coffee, a battered urn among them. An aquarium does the share. Can the story of a glass house full of water speak to him? He rolls forward, listening—"algae in the filter, bloated goldfish"—and takes a half-warm gulp and then another, until it hits him that the tank has stopped. A globule trembles, streaks, like sweat on ice.

"Hello, I'm a bowling ball and I'm an alcoholic." No one laughs.

GUILTY W/ AN EXPLANATION #2

The gun was, like, a prop. The bullets were symbols.
The blood—I hadn't thought that part through.

DEAR EZRA,

You died. Class dismissed. All that noise.
Well the Jews they're still with us—
one of 'em's my worst enemy:
                              me.
My plot to dictate the economy goes badly.
The elders screen my calls, ignore my counsel.
And goyim look down their button noses
at you, with your hypersonic booms and busts
        of meaning,
oy! your screwball scholarship du jour.
In their pacific eyes,
                        you may
be a bit of a Jew yourself.

Your schoolgirl crush on Mussolini—
poet's tears on seaside sand,
another day and no letter in return!
No wonder the sky ball leaks red fire
                        and drowns itself in the bay . . .

JACK LEVINE

The first time I was ever in art school I was an instructor. Thirty, out of the Army, with a painting already in the Met. Whose little boy was I gonna be?

Let me put it this way. With respect, I reject Matisse. But the feeling is out there that I am not allowed to do that. That's okay—he can go his way.

This is like a cry for freedom. Nobody should live under received opinion.

It was a very pivotal time. I assume everybody knows this historical patch, but it happened so long ago that nobody knows it but me. Nobody knows what it was like in '51.

Guston? You mean Fainting Phil? I met him the day I got out of the service. Barely out of my skivvies. I have to stop this. No reason to beat up on Phil. I shook hands with him at Eddie Millman's funeral. I could have thrown my hands up—but I shook his hand.

The market was flat. It's not that I was doing badly. Max Weber was doing badly. Matisse was selling at 20 times the price of Weber—because he was only an American. I was first married then, in a five-story walk-up on St. Marks Place, what they now call the East Village. A nice place, but also kind of a slum. My fancy friends were afraid to come visit. There's no reason on God's earth why I should take Matisse seriously. Except he's official. He's no Degas. Not even a Cezanne. But he's official. His position has to be protected.

She was a critic for, I don't remember the newspaper, and very upfront. One of them didn't like something she wrote, so he mailed her a used piece of toilet paper. I couldn't tell your students that. If you cross an avant garde artist with a thug, you'd see what I mean.

I was the same age as Motherwell. Still am. Can you be the same age as a corpse? And younger than de Kooning. And broad-minded. But punitive.

. . . more silos than I ever saw in my life. Out here jew is only a verb. How much farther to the airport?

My terrible sister who lives in Youngstown, she's the only one left. There were eight of us.

I have a confession to make. I loathe Jewish cooking, which makes it kind of difficult on High Holy Days—except of course Yom Kippur. Even then, though, afterwards . . .

MAY THE HEALING NOW BEGIN
to Bradley Smith, Holocaust Denier

We needed a Homeland.
Sorry.

A proud race took the fall.
Sue me.

Is this thing on?
I know you're out there,

I can hear you saluting.
I can hear you disinfecting.

–How far from here to Paris?
–About a four-day march. (Rimshot)

Enough already with my jokes.
The song and dance. The whole megillah.

From my lips to God's deaf ear:
it never happened.

(Lord, where is the broom with which
this many-tangled web to sweep away.)

Pure blood on bird-quick hands,
Eichmann's blood . . .

Idiot! I almost forgot
that "museum" in D.C.

And our imaginary martyr
who thought people are basically good,
maybe she should've met me!

Then there's you, Mr. Smith, on your cross,
hounded from pillar to post,

spat upon and shouted down
from Oshkosh to La Jolla.

Consider the case of Cassandra,
she who saw terror unseen,
whereas you unsee what was not.

Restitution! Ha!
Let this be a humble start.

◎   ◎   ◎

O how we danced in the firelight singing
THERE IN THE LAND OF OUR FATHERS—

GHAZAL OF THE LITERAL CONTRADICTION

I've broken numbered hearts, unspoken mumbled rules.
Faith comes in dirty colors, swims in summer schools.

Carbon copies curse the sun, dripping in a dream
where hard men curl and shiver, girls inside them waging duels.

Nothing changes into something else, simple-minded fact.
Switch places with a windowpane but don't mess with his tools.

One potato, two potato . . . That's plenty, no more spuds.
Famine's over, Emerald Eyes, we bathe in fossil fuels.

The wind machine blew hot then cold, then snuffed out every candle
in the cake-sweet-smelling night. Say act surprised, with jewels.

Don't make me do it, or deny it, or excavate. You dig?
We all got wound too tight that night: chokeholds on gasping spools.

THE RED WHEELBARROW OF FORTUNE

Pope John Paul is in Jordan
President Bill in Dakar
I'm here at SFO
Wishing on an airport bar

Wishing on an airport barmaid—
That would get me nowhere quick
Numbers lie to other numbers
Hand me down my swizzle stick

We are all in constant motion
Even as we sit and wait
Deep inside we tick like watches
Never stopping, always late

Children cheer a flag on fire
A car commercial ends
Hearts of darkness fill with light
The wind is up—*so much depends*...

WAR OF THE MINIMALIST

there is only one book

consisting of only one page

one word
one letter
one sound

there is only one reader

a distant relation
to the author

who is formulating
a defense

of
Otherness

ON BEING ASKED TO DEFINE *GHAZAL*

If your life swung in the balance
I would not feed you the answer.
Truth be told, I've looked it up
again and forgotten myself.
Nobody knows all the parts, wrapped and whole.
He told me to my face.
Of mispronunciation I stand
self-accused, unsorry.
(My way sounds like a dream.)

STATE POEM

Iowa lies halfway
Between Iowa and Iowa,
Surrounded on all sides by borders.
Main export: Iowans.

Hopefuls flock here every four.
As above the radar, so below:
This fertile ground of heavenseed,
Pheasants, distance, snow.

LEAVING OSCEOLA

It's bustling, here on the outskirts, at the junction of I-35 and two state highways—mostly locals, the rest of us en route but not so fast, special thanks to an early storm ahead of Halloween. Power outages, cars in ditches, snow plows keeping the arteries open, nonstop ringing off the hook. Always the same question. *Do you have electricity?* Except for the rare missing person. *Is Murray Davis here?* the cashier shouts across all that Formica toward the kitchen. *He was, yesterday morning.* (Scattered laughs.) Heartrending gaps in pies revolve. Touch glass, there'll be some left. Big parties at long tables—it takes three tickets to write up an order. Out front heavy branches twist and shout. An old green wagon erases itself beneath the **FAMILY TABLE** sign swaying like a toy in Mesmer's hand. Best Western, Super 8, Holiday Inn, filling up with travelers to and from Kansas City, Cedar Rapids, Minneapolis, Chicago throwing in the towel at 10:00 a.m. We turned back clocks last night. Watches too. Or didn't. More coffee? Church canceled in Des Moines. Denver shut down tight. Why not, with cream. LABOR GIVES VICE PREZ COLD SHOULDER I read over somebody's. He'll be by in three short years, firmly pumping these good people's hands, *counting on your support.* When I turned in, no sign of weather. The report was true, the man was right. In every direction: white.

HOUSEPAINT IS THICKER THAN WATER

I'm not going to let you hit my brother.
The older I get the bigger he looms,
Keith Castlebury, pumped, breathing fire,
pounding his fist on the open garage door,
demanding his check, *today.*
Hours earlier, he'd backed out, practically on all fours,
pulling his malfunctioning spray machine along.
Keith of the ex-wife and two small kids,
the songs he wrote and played us on cassette,
a joke to me, working for my brother,
back at home, Mike dead, paying nothing.
In my shining hour we stood him off together,
Jeff and I, to deny him his check,
partly from spite, for making us look bad.
Chip, legend has it, stayed inside the unit,
laughing like Mutley the Dog as it went down.
Keith left again, six two, a fuming chump.
(Later, the Labor Commission upheld his claim.)
Dunphy, big pink Dunphy, Jeff's old friend from swim team,
who bankrolled our little paint crew, never made 50.
His developer's heart gave out last year.
Thanks to him, they say, a thousand condos
bloomed in the Coachella Valley.
We faced Keith there in one of them,
my words etched in air, almost visible.
I locked in, thinking *what, fool, now—*
expecting to be flattened any second.
Now I know everybody is.

"I WAS A WORRIED CHILD . . ."

I was a worried child
My mother told me so
My worries kept me company
A kind of radio

I used to bite the other kids
That got the best of me
I'd open wide and bite their heads
They'd howl and then they'd flee

As soon as they got in the door
Their moms would call mine up
My brother likes to tell that one
I like to wish he'd stop

They say my brother's youngest
Acts something like I did
Another worried little guy
Knock wood he's never bit

These days I bite my lover
A quick one on the neck
At times I bite her harder
For love or for effect

I was a worried child
Now I'm a worried man
A great peace lies before me
Too clear to understand

UPON THE RASH OF RENAMINGS OF PUBLIC BUILDINGS IN HONOR OF RONALD REAGAN

I.

Two guitars, bass and drums,
Valéry up front singing lead,
of a stoned cold '70s Friday,
at midnight, on network tv.
Jeff's friends, five crazy Russians
a band with no name and one song,
from Berkeley, from Riga.
I thought Valéry was famous.
with his mustache and woodpile joke
–peasant outwits KGB, again,
and that story that barely made sense
–drunken Finns repair statue of Lenin.
(It must've been around this time the FBI
questioned Louise, about the letters
from Nancy Ling Perry: *Who is 'Lulu'?*
Patty Hearst. The SLA. Were those the days?)
Valéry pulled on the mic stand like Jagger
and Solzhenitsyn rolled into one:
OUT of the U.S.S.R.
You don't know how lucky you are, boys
OUT of the U.S.S.R.

II.

Valéry's Tale (Retold)

On the appointed day, in a central square,
where godless things went on,
the numberless throng gathered without choice
behind the Iron Curtain no one saw
or saw behind or ever thought to doubt,
for the unveiling of yet another monument
to Vladimir Ilyich Lenin,
pedastalled, larger than death—
in his outswept hand his worker's cap,
and to the puzzlement of all,
an identical cap on his head.

III.

In the streets the people were dancing,
reeling with frenzy and fury.
With lasso and pulley,
the victims, the herd,
took History's neck in their hands—
till the Man with Two Hats,
the Unwelcome Guest,
like a tree with dead shoots,
like a tree without roots,
like the hammer of heaven
came down.

CODA:

Jeff lives in Wisconsin now,
where black ice can kill you, it's hairy.
Berkeley is a state of mind,
and no one knows where is Valéry.

ON UNDERTAKING THE *ODYSSEY* AT 42 ABOARD THE COAST STARLIGHT SOUTHBOUND

Disguised as ragged Mentes, Pallas Athena
has told her white lies to Telemachus
(in the Robert Fagles translation, guaranteed
by *People* magazine "to make you tune out
the Smashing Pumpkins and turn off *Melrose Place*").
Her words turn on a dime, fool's gold to gold:
His father is alive and will return.
                                        The suitors,
dripping meat juice, help themselves to palace wine.
Penelope is running out of guile.
Telemachus must set sail in the morning—

as the On-Board Entertainer plants herself
in the center of the Observation Car
and strums her ukulele:

    "Sing along . . ."

     This Old Man
     Wabash Cannonball
     I Been Workin' On The Railroad
     Someone's In The Kitchen With Dinah
     Oh Susannah
     You Are My Sunshine
     He's Got The Whole World In His Hands
     Home On The Range

(Did she swallow an American Songbag?
Is the whole thing coming back up?)

Christ, they want an encore:

Bicycle Built For Two

Lord have mercy, she's through.
Furrowed fields sail past, someone says: Tomato.
A superfan announces: 20-14, Minnesota.

◎   ◎   ◎

No more Telemachus than Bus Riley,
no man's king, no child's hero,
still I am always returning:

The old man—a law unto himself—
must have read Homer in Latin.
Fatherless, big-city poor,
he won the gold medal at Central.
A pin boy from West Philadelphia
nursemaids a wife who lies dying,
my sweet young-once only mother,
a shell of bone and pain,
kitten-weak, wearing a great-grandma mask.
(I look like an anarchist uncle.)
My sunny-side mother, who sang
How Much Is That Doggy In The Window
doing dinner dishes for six,
and bade her last-born to practice piano—
"You'll be popular at parties."
I went down another road entirely,
lost more often than not, under an ancient spell.

OUR FATHER

Tired by eleven a.m.,
drapes drawn to permanent dusk,
with a bib of newsprint he sleeps in his chair
next to the big unmade bed
where Parkinson's thinned her to nothing.
The old shouter won't waste away,
though he might burst out of disgust,
at the charlatans peddling bunk,
turning Science on its ear,
like chiropractors. Worse.
Let alone the lawyer who took
twelve days to return his call.

Retired but still on staff,
he eats at the doctor's lounge
wearing a hollow-leg grin,
ten slices of bacon, all free.
Unlike the silver seniors
in elastic on the train
he'll never "thank the Good Lord"
on a mat in a gym.

He buys mineral rocks from tv
for his ribbon of garden.
Homecomings, laundry, his letters
clipped out of the *Desert Sun* . . .
He has lived to see Yasser Arafat
shaking the president's hand,
the Dow Jones pass 10,000 on the run.

By early afternoon he's humming away,
King of Matinees at the Courtyard 6.

LARKINESQUE

Cars starting hours before dawn
wake up and smell the gasoline, pal
arouse me and who else
within earshot, as they slide out of
their bed-sized slots
away from and toward other light,
other darkness. Beating the rush?
Running cold? Flush with new or dead love?

Off goes the switch, away the pen,
and it's goodbye yellow chair, green formica
kitchen table. The cats are up now, crunchingly so.
Wake up and smell the exhaustion, pal,
of comings and goings on, of the face
in the bathroom mirror, night closing in all around,
silent compacter of trash and of treasure alike.

TRAFFIC REPORT

A stump of a man
with a crick in his neck

barrels on through
white moss and mesh sack

on foot in slow motion.
This damn intersection

mutters Magoo
needs a real stoplight.

Still-cooling, a self-
contained world bops by,

plugged in,
talk-singing along.

HONK HONK
In the back seat in over-

sized glasses
a boy points out the window

look look
at the silly sad billy goat goose

momma look
rubbing his fat little neck.

BLUE DOOM

Gimme a sec, said the comma. Roger that, a stone-faced period replied. In my day, fumed Count Ampersand, elegance had clout, a symbol meant one thing. Inverted, in itals, a question mark exhaled a Spanish sigh. Stow it, fancy pants!! chimed the exclamation twins, subtle as a brace of billy clubs. Who, piped up a footnote, makes the effort anymore. Down here. Further. I'll explain...

Brackets rocked in mirrored shades of laughter. The dollar jumped, then fell. Ramrod straight quotation marks played doormen: open, close. Plus or minus, the whole keyboard piled on. Even as the backspace key advanced unstated threats, came a shadow, came a scratch from on high—diagonal, decisive, graphite, blue.

All roads lead to silence, none to peace.

WHITE HEAT

Shot up with seizure-inducing photons in his sleep, Philip K. Dick embarked on his next book. A ream of paper, a dependable machine. Typing dark to dark in clatter-code. Looking for his dead twin sister. Waking at his desk. Converting pulp to precious metal with his Will. Accruing royalties he would need a time machine to spend. Finding God one character at a time.

GREEN GLASS

for Kerouac

In a daze I stumbled through a summer song. Love lusted for Itself, pent up inside the prison of the heart. To dig, to tap, spoon by spoon to tunnel—practice patience—to . . . escape. The chase! The hunt! The river! Boss Glass-Darkly, let your Klieg Light shine! Hounds, lead on. And Love, the model prisoner? Gone daddy, gone daddy gone, unscented and approaching the state line, in the woods not full of wardens (just this once), Brother Jack.

THE ETERNAL PRESENT

8:48 a.m. 62 degrees.
The parking lots are full, the message was delivered,
it's not about to rain and I'm not about to cry.

The water shortage ended years ago.
Now it's pouring, only only in here.
The Wu Le Food Co. is dry as a bone,

dry as a blow-dried bone.
Our happy home is green and lush
as Forest Lawn. Even her hair cascades.

Winter passes like a meal
that sits and hardens.
Six sides of nowhere face each other down

in this sewer of stopwatch light.
Boo! Murdered dreams! A cobra in a basket,
the sea conceals its fangs,

and she's gone, climbing down
her own dark fall. Who could stand
one more minute that damp tower, the self?

Warm-winded night. She's back,
summer smoke with a stylish new bob
much too short to twine.

All heaven breaks loose in the basement.
Pressed roses float to freedom.
Don't we all?

NOTES & ACKNOWLEDGEMENTS

Detours on the road to print took long enough that Carl Rakosi, who contributed an encomium, passed away in the interim, at the age of 100. Thanks to Brian Kaufman, this book was resurrected and reconfigured subtly but significantly over the past year.

"The New Library": Nicholson Baker and Walter Biller got to the bottom of the situation. Bleep: Ken Dowlin.

"The World Stage": King Hussein of Jordan; Queen Noor.

"Dysfunctional Don": Sam Giancana.

"The Attorney Arrives At His Office On April 16th": For years I worked for a lawyer, next to an CPA firm; the narrator was invented from whole cloth.

NUMBER NINE: A Presidential Suite: Seemingly continuous election cycles feel so important at the time. Looking back, Roman emperors, most of them decidedly minor, come to mind.

"Going Public": In the 1960s, Carol Doda famously had her breasts enhanced and graced the Condor Club in North Beach. She still performs, with The Lucky Stiffs.

"Upon The Rash Of Renamings Of Public Buildings In Honor Of Ronald Reagan": Valéry Saifdumov and Co. performed live once, on *Midnight Special*. Not to be confused with the legendary Valéry Gaina.

These poems or earlier versions appeared in:

Artillery, Poet & Critic, Ambit (U.K.), *THE SHOp* (Ireland), *The Red Wheelbarrow* (Scotland), *Evergreen Review, Dust Congress, Coe Review, The Temple, Processed World, Oxygen, Quiddity, Chiron Review, Comfusion Review, Curbside Review, WordWrights, Free Lunch, FUCK!, Poesy, Instant City, S.F. Herald, Cups, Architrave, Red Booth Review, Troubadour, The Ghazal Page, Pith, Fogged Clarity, Scissors and Spackle, Conclave: A Journal of Character, Tenement Block Review* (UK).

"Dysfunctional Don" and "The Attorney Arrives At His Office On April 16th" appeared in *Poetry* (Chicago).

"Dear Ezra," previously appeared in *Twilight of the Male Ego* (Tsunami Inc., Walla Walla, WA, 2002).

Individual poems appeared in the following anthologies:

The Outlaw Bible of American Poetry (Thunder's Mouth); *Nepotism* (Parthenon West/Comfusion); *It's All Good* (Manic D Press).

Broadsides of the following poems were issued by:

"Washington, D.C., 1863" (Turkey Press, Isla Vista, CA, as part of its Folded Broadside series, 2013);

"Memo To Wordsworth" (Poor Souls Press, Millbrae, CA, 2013);

"Wild Wild Ways" (David Hurst Publication Design, Chico, CA, 2013);

"Lester Rogers" (Pride of Tacoma Press, Santa Barbara, CA, 2005).

Big Thanks Goes Out To:

Chip Close (R.I.P.), Jon Cone, Edwin Dobb, Andy Fox, Jeff Jensen, John Lane, M. Vincent Perez, Albert Sgambati, Mel C. Thompson—for editorial assistance above and beyond; Neal Bowers, Joie Cook (R.I.P.), Paul Fericano, Stephanie Finch, November Garcia, Jeremy Gaulke, Chas Hansen, Bob Higgins, Brenda Hillman, Thaddeus Homan, J.R. Horsting, Dave Hurst, John T. Philipsborn, Charles Potts, Chuck Prophet, Harry Reese, Sandra Liddell Reese, Tom Stolmar, John Tottenham, Rachel Travers—for abundant and individual cause; Brian Kaufman, Karen Green, and everyone behind the scenes at Anvil; and, through and through, Colette.

ABOUT THE AUTHOR

klipschutz (pen name of Kurt Lipschutz) is a poet, songwriter and occasional freelance journalist. Born in Indio, California, he has lived in San Francisco for thirty years, where he shares an apartment with his wife Colette Jappy and three cats. His work has appeared in periodicals in the U.S., Canada, the U.K., Ireland and France, and numerous anthologies, as well as the previous collections *Twilight of the Male Ego, The Good Neighbor Policy,* and *The Erection of Scaffolding for the Re-Painting of Heaven by the Lowest Bidder.* He has co-penned over a hundred songs, chiefly with Chuck Prophet, including the recent *Temple Beautiful.* In 2006 his imprint Luddite Kingdom Press issued the limited edition collectible *All Roads. . . But This One.* Beyond high school, he is an autodidact.